EDU(
A CRITIQUE OF CURRENT
POLICY

Impact No.1

Educational Assessment: a critique of current policy

BY ANDREW DAVIS

Edited by John White

Published by the Philosophy of Education Society of Great Britain

First published in 1999 by the
Philosophy of Education Society of Great Britain

© Philosophy of Education Society of Great Britain

Distributed by Business and Medical Book Centre
9 Headlands Business Park
Ringwood, Hants BH24 3PB

British Library Cataloguing in Publication Data:
a catalogue record for this publication is
available from the British Library

ISBN 0-902227-02-5

Produced in Great Britain by
Reprographic Services
Institute of Education University of London

Printed by Formara Limited
16 The Candlemakers, Temple Farm Industrial Estate, Southend on Sea, Essex SS2 5RX

P1/0001-IMPACT No1-0999

CONTENTS

	page
Editorial introduction	vii

Overview
Educational Assessment: 1
A critique of current policy

1. Raising standards 5

2. Teaching to the test 14

3. The official language of the 19
   National Curriculum and
   of the 'Standards' laid down
   for Newly Qualified Teachers

4. Using assessment to hold 25
   schools and teachers to
   account

5. Prescribing teaching 29
   methods

6. OFSTED inspections 34

7. Realistic accountability: can 42
   we still hold teachers and
   schools to account?
   If so how, and why?

   References 48

THE IMPACT EDITORIAL TEAM

Professor John White
(Editor)
Institute of Education
University of London

Professor Christopher Winch
(Deputy Editor)
University College
Northampton

Richard Smith,
University of Durham
Editor of the *Journal of Philosophy of Education*

Dr Paul Standish
University of Dundee
Assistant Editor of the
Journal of Philosophy of Education

EDITORIAL INTRODUCTION

Educational Assessment - a Critique of Current Policy by Andrew Davis is the first pamphlet in the new IMPACT series, an initiative of the Philosophy of Education Society of Great Britain. The purpose of the series is to bring philosophical perspectives to bear on current UK education policy.

What lies behind the IMPACT initiative? It arises out of the conviction that there are philosophical dimensions to education policy, whether policy makers see them or not. Even if they are aware of them in a general way, most are not trained philosophers and cannot be expected to see implications and ramifications that a philosopher would see. The cost of not perceiving these implications, as Andrew Davis's paper admirably illustrates, is that policies may end up muddled or even self-contradictory.

Philosophers interested in education have not always had a good press. Over the last two decades they have been attacked, along with educationists from other disciplines, as spanners in the works of educational progress, or in Kenneth Clarke's elegant words as 'barmy theorists'. This is not the place to lick old wounds: not least because there have been signs in the last couple of years that the political climate for philosophy is changing. National policy makers are becoming more attentive to deeper issues affecting education issues that have philosophical dimensions.

Citizenship education, for instance, is now on the agenda. After 2000 Citizenship is due to become a new compulsory foundation subject of the National Curriculum at key stages 3 and 4. But what is it to learn to be a citizen? This is not so easy a question to answer as, say, 'what is it to learn arithmetic?' It takes one into the nature of democracy, of liberalism, of alternatives to these, of rights, of values like fairness, freedom, attachment to community. It raises questions also about the abilities and attitudes, skills and understanding that people need in order to live well as citizens now and the future. These are all topics where it is easy to lose one's way in a labyrinth of linked ideas, to end up in confusion or in a spurning of abstract reflection in the interests of getting something done. That philosophy has a crucial role to play in helping us to get clear about these matters was recognised by the appointment of a political philosopher, Professor Bernard Crick, to chair the Advisory Group on Education for Citizenship and the Teaching of Democracy in Schools which reported in 1998.

There are other recent examples of philosophical participation. It has been welcomed in the work of the Qualifications and Curriculum Authority on the aims of the National Curriculum after 2000, and in problems faced by the National Advisory Committee on Creative and Cultural Education over the concepts of creativity and imagination. In addition, there is a new interest in government circles in critical thinking.

Whether all this adds up to a definite trend towards taking philosophical considerations into account is not yet clear. This is where IMPACT plays a crucial role. Its short, incisive papers are written expressly with policy-makers and practitioners in mind, avoiding technical terms and an over-involvement in academic debates. The papers provide both philosophical rigour and also signposts towards more scholarly territory for those who want to explore the issues further. Andrew Davis's paper which launches the series expertly treads this fine line between accessibility and rigour.

Further IMPACT papers will be published on average once every two or three months. At the time of writing, they are taking shape on the wordprocessors of both general philosophers and professional philosophers of education. Forthcoming pamphlets will discuss such topical issues as: post-16 vocational education; education and equality with special reference to school admissions; the new National Curriculum and its aims; citizenship education; performance related pay; good teaching; sex education; personal, social and health education; and the place of modern languages in the curriculum. A full list of topics due to appear soon after the millennium will be found at the end of this pamphlet.

Also at the end of every pamphlet, including this one, there is a list of suggestions for further reading. This enables readers to examine opposing, or simply alternative, arguments on the same issues.

Each IMPACT paper expresses the ideas of its author only. It does not represent the view of the Philosophy of Education Society of Great Britain. There is indeed, no such single view. PESGB contains some 500 members whose ideas and political allegiances are widely disparate.

The author of this first IMPACT paper, Dr Andrew Davis, is Lecturer in Education at the School of Education, University of Durham. His work on assessment in recent years has rapidly established him as one of the national leaders in this field. His full-length treatment of the topic appeared in his philosophical monograph *The Limits of Educational Assessment* (Oxford, Blackwell, 1998). Andrew Davis is excellently qualified to write on this topic. He is both a lucid and scholarly philosopher and has also had many years experience as a primary teacher and lecturer in primary education, with a special interest in primary mathematics. It was because of this combination of qualities, along with their admiration for his monograph on assessment, that the IMPACT editorial team were delighted to invite him to launch our pamphlet series.

Andrew Davis shows that the rigorous systems now in place for assessing pupils at school, their teachers and teachers-in-training are supposed to be in the service of raising educational standards partly so that Britain can compete more effectively in the global marketplace. But, given that this goal is desirable, do these systems constitute an intelligent way of trying to achieve it?

It is impossible to answer this question without examining the abilities which assessment systems purport to assess and seeing whether they can *in principle* assess them. This is not an empirical matter for social science to determine. It is not a question of observing a great number of assessment schemes and seeing whether they do in fact measure up to what they are supposed to accomplish. There is a prior task. That is to see whether it *makes sense* to claim that the assessment schemes can do this. Andrew Davis's paper explores this question and finds below the surface what he takes to be serious contradictions. He suggests that the present assessment system be dismantled in favour of a more defensible alternative which he outlines in the final section of the paper.

John White
August 1999

Educational Assessment: a critique of current policy

Introduction

This pamphlet develops six complaints about current educational assessment policy. If these complaints are justified, the policy threatens to damage the interests of pupils, the viability of the British economy and the chances of recruiting and maintaining a high quality teaching force.

The six complaints are first summarised before being explained in detail.

1. Raising Standards is being equated with improving test performance

The Government is very anxious about the relative performance of British pupils in international tests of numeracy and literacy.

Evidently it thinks that good test performance is associated with a successful industrial economy. We are told that examination results must improve. David Blunkett will resign if the Literacy and Numeracy targets are not met by 2002. More than 75% of Year 6 children must reach level 4 or better in mathematics, and more than 80% must achieve this in English. Children's 'levels' will be measured by the statutory Standard Assessment Tasks (SATs). This whole exercise is described as 'raising standards' in education.

The pamphlet argues that the description 'raising standards' is a mistake. It is not a synonym for improving examination performance. A competitive industrial economy needs employees who can both communicate and listen, make flexible and intelligent use of their knowledge and skills, work effectively with others and who are suitably motivated. These qualities cannot be tested by examinations. Indeed the pressure to improve test performance may reduce the likelihood of children developing these traits.

2. *Current policies encourage teaching to the test and this distorts the curriculum*

Teaching to the test is not a new problem. However, it has been greatly exacerbated by recent Government policy that relies heavily on assessment to make schools and teachers accountable for the cost of education. The pamphlet explores in some detail the difficulties this raises for any attempts to improve the 'real learning' of pupils. Teaching to the test distorts and restricts learning.

3. Using standardised language in the National Curriculum and in the Standards for Newly Qualified Teachers for accountability purposes distorts learning

Teachers are being held to account for the learning outcomes of their pupils, and these are being described in the officially sanctioned language of the National Curriculum. Equally, teacher trainers are being held to account for the Standards laid down for Newly Qualified Teachers. These Standards are couched in the terminology of DfEE Circular 14/98.

For teachers, schools or Higher Education Institutions to be compared fairly, the approved languages need a genuine national currency. They must be used with a consistent meaning. It is argued here that this is only possible if they describe children's or teachers' mastery of narrow skills in a restricted range of contexts. Yet accountability in education should surely extend beyond a concern with such narrow skills.

4. Using assessment to hold schools and teachers to account is unjust

Educational assessment, mainly in the form of public examinations and tests, is being used by politicians to hold schools and teachers to account. Judgements are made about whether value for money is being offered. Judgements of the quality of schools and even of individual teachers are being derived from the results of assessment. Attempts to make the comparisons fairer by using value added measures are discussed. It is concluded that these attempts are bound to fail.

5. Teachers are being told how to teach and yet are still being held to account for their pupils' learning

Increasingly teachers are being required by the DfEE or other Government-backed agencies to teach in specified ways, in addition to being held to account for the learning achieved by their pupils. This pamphlet argues that in many cases such prescription of teaching methods is EITHER empty OR incompatible with holding schools and teachers to account for pupil learning.

6. OFSTED inspections cannot accurately detect teaching quality

OFSTED claims to be able to assess the quality of teaching in schools and Higher Education Institutions. Heads and LEA personnel are going to have to judge the quality of teaching in order that 'fast track' school staff may be awarded the pay rises made so much of by New Labour. This pamphlet argues that inspectors are not in a position to judge 'effective' teaching defined as that which brings about learning in the lessons they observe. What is actually going on during inspections is something rather different. OFSTED is in fact assuming that it is generally known which teaching methods maximise pupil learning, and that the employment of these methods may be readily detected on the basis of limited observation. These assumptions are mistaken.

1
Raising Standards

> *Raising Standards is being equated with improving test performance.*

Knowledge worth having

I need knowledge, understanding and skills of various kinds to survive in my daily life and also at work. Such knowledge must be *connected* in my mind in many ways to other things I know. If not, it may be 'in' my mind without being understood. I will be unable to use or apply it. Perhaps all I can do is answer a test question correctly.

Suppose I 'know' that Michael Faraday discovered the dynamo. Unless I also am aware of other facts about dynamos, electricity, science in general, the Victorian era, and appreciate the links between these and my Michael Faraday material, I can do nothing with the latter except to regurgitate it on demand. Evidently the linkage between a specific piece of knowledge and other knowledge will not be an all-or-nothing affair. It will be a matter of degree. As pupils learn and mature we would expect the 'connectedness' of their knowledge to develop in accuracy, comprehensiveness and sophistication.

Knowledge that enables me to function as an adult may be used and applied flexibly in a range of contexts. I read tax forms, information on packages in shops, books, instructions and on-screen information from a database or the Internet. I write notes for my milkman, application forms for jobs and letters to my friends and relatives. I extract the meaning from instruction manuals and I enter material sensibly in a computer database. Circumstances will draw on my literacy skills in very different ways.

I calculate mentally, sometimes rounding up or down to produce an approximate answer that may be all that is needed. On encountering a problem requiring some arithmetic, I recognise whether to add, subtract, multiply or divide, or indeed to perform the appropriate combination of these operations. When numbers are complicated, or there are many of them, I may use a calculator or computer. Before I calculate, I have a rough idea of the answer. This helps me to identify possible slips, whether in my mental arithmetic or in my use of calculator or computer. In order to perform intelligent estimates and to select appropriate operations I need to appreciate the links between addition and subtraction, multiplication and division, and how the whole number system works.

Both literacy and numeracy also depend for their successful application upon pupils developing a range of relevant *practical* skills. These are evidently quite crucial. It would be perfectly possible to turn out pupils who are theoretically literate and numerate but who could not actually apply their knowledge because of their practical inadequacies.

To sum up, I cannot be intelligently literate and numerate unless I have linked relevant knowledge and concepts in my mind. Arguably Government should assume that tests and examinations can probe whether pupils are at least beginning to form such connections. Failing this, it ought to presuppose that whatever is involved in preparing for tests is *strongly associated* with the making of such connections. Further, Government must hold that pupils can use this connected knowledge in adulthood in the ways described. Otherwise improving examination performance can have little to do with 'raising standards'. I now raise objections to each of these assumptions.

First of all, written tests cannot properly assess the extent of candidates' 'connected' knowledge. They fail to discriminate between two categories of pupils:

1. those who have 'learned up' particular sets of facts or specific skills but who can only use them efficiently in examination contexts, and

2. those who are developing a richer, more connected knowledge, in the light of which they can obtain satisfactory test scores.

Candidates who learn up content for the sake of the test are likely to assimilate a body of material that is isolated from the rest of what they know. Such knowledge is not usable and applicable in a range of contexts. This is partly because it is not thoroughly understood. As we have just seen, flexibility of application depends on knowledge being 'connected up' in the mind in the right kind of way.

Incidentally, written tests by definition fail to check whether pupils have appropriate *practical* skills. After early attempts to make some SATs include a range of practical activities, we have retreated to paper and pencil tasks. The forays into practical work were said to be too time-consuming. Of course, some public examinations do include practical elements. Yet these tests cannot discriminate between pupils who are trained up to be able to exercise a particular practical skill in the examination room, and pupils who can make use of this skill in a much wider range of contexts.

The second assumption underlying the identification of 'raising standards' with improving test scores is that better test preparation and performance eventually transfer to similar or related contexts encountered in daily life and in the work place. It also must include the thought that pupils will do at least adequately *in contexts that are less closely related* but still 'relevant'. To support such thinking we need the premiss that the improvement of test scores and the associated teaching is linked to the development of 'connected' knowledge. Unless all this is so, 'raising standards' becomes a very thin and uninspiring objective. It merely covers performance in school tests.

There is considerable empirical evidence[1] that pupils who succeed in given contexts may well not perform as well in others that we would regard as similar or involving the same knowledge, skill or competence. For instance, seemingly trivial differences in the way mathematical tasks are presented can make significant differences to success rates even where the 'same' arithmetical operation would seem to be demanded. This is not to say that transfer never occurs. Of course it does. Indeed, without it some would argue that learning could scarcely go on.

However, the difficulties about transfer are profound, and we need to look beyond the empirical evidence that is merely the surface of the problem. The difficulties stem from our thinking about *sameness* and *similarity* when applied to human performance, knowledge and the contexts in which it may be displayed. For instance, we may think that if a pupil does well in a school maths test she will also be able to do similar mathematics in other contexts. The implications of her maths test results seem weaker for her performance on scientific tasks, because they are felt to resemble the school mathematics tasks less closely. We may judge that there are no implications for her chances with a swimming task, since swimming is not similar to mathematics in any way. We assume that questions of similarity are 'objective' and can be settled scientifically in some sense.

Unfortunately, similarity lacks this status in human and social contexts. Judgements about whether one human action, performance or context is similar to another reflect the purposes of the judges. Such judgements are not *objectively* right or wrong. That is to say, they differ from, for instance, a claim about whether one rock is made of the same elements as another. Scientists can discover the constituents of the rock. Either it is or it is not made of the same elements. The lack of 'scientific' objectivity in similarity judgements about human activity explains at least in part why transfer is so unreliable.

Identifying 'raising standards' with improving test performance assumes that, for instance, better performance in English examinations means enhanced English in real-life contexts. Improving the results of mathematics tests is supposed to be significantly related to later success in the mathematical challenges of the work place. Many policy makers will feel that these links are just obvious. However, note just how much reliance they are apparently placing on the existence of very strong associations between test performance in a subject and its real life applications. Such confidence seems to appeal to a robust and 'objective' notion of similarity that is not actually available.

Another way of looking at this issue is through an examination of the work we try to do with terms such as 'ability', 'skill' or 'competence'. It is easy to coin phrases that appear to refer to psychological items of these kinds. Examples include 'critical thinking skills', 'problem solving abilities' and 'caring skills'. We hope that these phrases will refer to assets which people can acquire and retain, just as the phrase 'ball throwing ability' apparently can. We see Jones throwing balls in various situations, and conclude that he has the ability to throw a ball. This implies that he will succeed in throwing balls on future occasions if the circumstances are right and he wants to. That is, the ball-throwing is expected to transfer to future occasions. Of course, confidence would decline if he were being asked to throw under water, or to throw a metal ball weighing 5 kg. Our trust in our transfer predictions is reasonably grounded on the observability of Jones's performances, the judgement that his skills are explicable in terms of adequately functioning musculature, senses and brain, and the assumption that these physical features are stable in the short and medium term.

Many educational uses of 'ability', 'skill' or 'competence' try to pick out achievements that are far more elusive than 'ball-throwing ability'. We need to understand in some detail the difficulties here. A classic example is provided by 'problem solving ability'. Perhaps Jane, a Year-11 pupil, cleans a sparking plug in the car in the school engineering workshop, replaces a fuse in an electric soldering iron, charges a flat battery in the school video camera and helps a teacher to remember where he left his reading glasses. Each of these might be described as practical problem-solving. So we might say that Jane has a practical problem-solving ability (Davis 1988).

What does our judgement mean? On one interpretation we may be talking about Jane's customary enthusiasm for practical tasks, the fact that she wastes no time in embarking on them, and that she rarely if ever leaves a job half done. In short, we may be attributing to her a positive attitude to practical tasks. On a second interpretation we are merely summarising previous achievements and so talk of a problem-solving ability is superficial but harmless. These two interpretations are not mutually exclusive.

Any attempt made to take the idea of problem-solving ability more seriously, and to predict future successes in virtue of Jane's possession of some kind of 'problem-solving muscle', should be treated with scepticism. For there need be nothing common to Jane's various problem-solvings. If we exclude Jane's attitude to solving problems as an explanation of her successes, we have no other reason to predict future achievements in this regard. The knowledge and understanding on which she would draw could involve a wide range of subject matter. No limits could be set on the physical actions that might figure. Indeed some problems can be 'solved' without performing any physical actions at all. The invention of the phrase 'problem solving ability' in effect *seeks to conjure into existence a psychological trait that will guarantee that transfer will occur.*

Many National Curriculum statements describing pupil achievement need to invoke these kinds of mythological abilities or competences, if we take the language seriously. [That] 'pupils use a range of sentence structures and varied vocabulary' (DFE 1995b) implies, surely, that pupils can do this in a range of contexts and within a variety of different types of writing. Or consider the claim that pupils 'use abstract ideas in descriptions and explanations, such as electric current being a flow of charge, the sum of several forces determining changes in the direction or the speed of movement of an object, or wind and waves being energy resources available for use' (DFE 1995a). This characterisation clearly implies a *general* competence. Certainly *examples* are given, but the implication is that pupils could use abstract ideas in connection with a whole range of scientific content.

Analysis of a simple mathematical case may well help to drive this point home. At first sight, mathematics may appear to be relatively cut and dried, and the business of attributing to pupils basic numeracy skills perfectly straightforward in comparison with problem-solving or advanced writing skills. Now consider the alleged ability to subtract. A pupil can give the correct answer whenever she is given 12-5 in written symbolic form. However, a 'subtraction competence' would need to amount to rather more than this. Perhaps she also ought to succeed when the subtraction is presented vertically. Now suppose we ask her the question in conversation rather than writing it for her. Imagine that terms other than 'take away' are used. How will she respond to 'subtract', 'minus' or 'difference'? So far, we have restricted ourselves to the subtraction of one particular number from another. But of course, she needs to be able to deal with the subtraction of *any* numbers. Do we have an upper limit in mind? What about including an example such as 5 -12? Imagine that we turn aside from giving her subtraction problems in the abstract, and instead suggest challenges in realistic contexts that require subtraction of some kind to be solved.

Perhaps we are confident that she will be able to meet all these challenges. Any such confidence cannot be justified without certain convictions about transfer, these beliefs in turn perhaps buttressed by the thought that our pupil has some kind of underlying 'subtraction muscle'. (Obviously we do not use the term 'subtraction muscle'. It is simply a vivid phrase that captures the type of thinking at work here.) Yet much of this whole story depends on a kind of unobtainable clarity and objectivity about 'same' and 'similar'. We assert, for instance, that what must go on to solve 5-12 is 'similar' in some sense to that which must take place to solve 10-6. However, mere assertion will not spirit subtraction abilities into existence, nor bring about transfer just because the knowledge or operation required *seems* so similar.

It follows from the problems about transfer and the mythology of abilities, competences and skills in education that the global identification of 'raising standards' with improving test performance cannot be justified. The effect of improving examination results on the qualities pupils will later exhibit as adults is far from obvious. In fact it may be argued that school curricula will be so dominated by test-related practice that activities involving working with others, using imagination, and coming to understand the way a democratic society functions will be side-lined. Further, driving up school test scores in literacy and numeracy need not mean more literate and numerate employees. In the long run we may actually damage the very economy that the 'basics' were supposed to help.

One objection to my line of argument runs as follows. It concedes that adults need knowledge that they can use and apply. It goes on to admit that this is something to do with the degree to which they understand what they know, or the way all the different knowledge elements they possess are properly connected together in their minds.

However it then recalls the point made above: connectedness is a matter of degree. Pupils cannot be expected to make all these connections at once. This understanding will develop gradually, as will the 'transfer' to a wider range of contexts. So the fact that written tests and examinations cannot detect it at school is not a problem after all.

I believe this whole line of thinking simply side-steps the issue I have raised about similarity judgements and human performance. We lack a comprehensive justification for the *kinds* of activities currently dominating the curriculum especially at the primary stage, many of which seek to prepare pupils for tests and examinations. For all we know, significant curriculum time given to the arts might contribute to the flexible and intelligent literacy and numeracy required of adults in the third millennium at least as much as teaching to the literacy and numeracy tests. Once we lose confidence in, for example the transparency of the relationship between the English of SATs preparation and the English demanded by the workplace we can consider returning to a richer conception of primary school English. We can once more extend a welcome to drama and poetry. Or again, we might spend a little less time on preparing for that mathematics test, and devote it instead to music and the arts. Claims about the so-called 'Mozart Effect'[2] have been widespread in the last year or so. Another oddity is that it has recently been reported that primary children subjected to versions of the 'numeracy hour' seemed to improve at English. (TES 1999) None of this is the least surprising, of course, once we grasp the problematic character of similarity judgements about human performance and knowledge.

2
Teaching to the test

> *Current policies encourage teaching to the test and this distorts the curriculum.*

Teaching to the test is not a new problem. However, it may be thought that modern examination procedures can now avoid it. To circumvent the well-worn possibility of candidates and teachers narrowing teaching and learning in order to meet the demands of the tests, examiners over time may offer a *wide range* of either written or practical problems. For example, in their construction of Key Stage 2 Maths SATs the QCA deliberately alters the way in which problems are presented from one year to the next. It recommends that teachers prepare children by practising in varying formats and contexts:

> Teachers need to ... teach both informal and standard methods, using all four operations ... to enable children to select appropriate strategies for questions presented in a variety of ways and situations. (QCA 1998:29)

I now show that there are serious objections to this strategy for avoiding the 'teaching to the test' problem. I argue that a policy of deliberate variation will introduce an element of luck into the final test grades. Let us consider this point in detail.

Tests ought to detect candidates' knowledge and understanding with some accuracy and consistency. Pupils with similar levels of knowledge ought to obtain equivalent scores. However, candidates' scores may differ simply according to whether chance favours them with question types with which they are familiar. The test results will not necessarily reflect *real* discrepancies in knowledge and understanding between one candidate and another. In short, well-intentioned QCA policies may result in unfair tests. Of course no test is completely fair, but we must constantly bear in mind that the results of these tests are being used to inform judgements about the quality of teachers and schools.

Admittedly, in some subjects and at some levels the ways of asking candidates about the relevant knowledge are strictly limited. Thus teachers can rehearse their pupils in all the variants, and the element of luck will be ruled out. In other cases there is apparently no limit to the number of possible task variants. Each year inventive examiners can create something new. Surely an element of luck within tests *used for accountability purposes* is wholly unacceptable.

Test designers may suggest that I have missed the point. They actually have an enlightened view of proper educational objectives, and they seek to encourage teachers to pursue these by varying question types from one year to the next. Their notion of a proper educational objective includes the kind of connectedness in knowledge and understanding that I have claimed is essential for adult functioning. (They are unlikely to characterise it in terms of 'connectedness' but this idea could be implicit in their thinking.) Once a rich understanding is achieved, their argument goes on, pupils will be able to *transfer* from the contexts in which they have been taught to new types. At first, they will urge, pupils only succeed in contexts that closely resemble the ones in which they have been taught. However, with the right variety of diet, and given effective teaching over a sufficient period, children will be able to succeed in anything that the examiners can throw at them. For example, in the first instance pupils can add numbers presented horizontally, or add with counters, or add when given written problems involving the terms 'plus' or 'how many altogether'. The teacher will gently bombard the pupils with a range of addition tasks. The day will dawn when virtually any problem that involves addition regardless of format will be solved successfully by the pupils. Or so we may be told.

However, we have already seen that there is much less about the idea of similarity than meets the eye. Pupils often cannot reach a point where we can be reasonably confident about the 'kinds' of things they can do. This is true even of a simple operation such as addition. Any belief to the contrary rests on the kinds of convictions about transfer and appeals to fictional mental traits so comprehensively criticised in the previous section.

This brings me to a discussion of a second major problem connected with teaching to the test. It concerns how both teachers and pupils actually view the nature of the knowledge and understanding being taught. It is often suggested that teachers and pupils ought to be as explicit and as clear as possible about the knowledge and skills on which the lesson is focusing. This is certainly a theme of OFSTED research reports and of school inspection reports. For instance:

> In the best examples, teachers began by explaining the objectives of the lesson to the class. They referred back to these objectives throughout the lesson, for example when drawing the pupils together after 10 or 15 minutes to work on a new concept or to clarify or reinforce key teaching points. (OFSTED 1998a:11)

Or

> In the best lessons teachers make it clear to pupils what it is they are to learn ... (OFSTED 1998b:16)

Now teachers constrained by the pressures of league tables may actually be intending to teach pupils a limited range of closely-defined performances. (If test designers refrain from inventing new types of questions each year teachers will always know in advance about the kinds of tasks in which their pupils must eventually succeed. After all, as tests, the predictable variety are fairer as accountability devices even if they are potentially more damaging to the curriculum.) So, if OFSTED is right, teachers ought to maximise their chances of obtaining what they want from their pupils by sharing with their pupils these short-term learning objectives.

However, this transmits to the pupils the idea that to learn is to acquire a specific set of procedures, namely those required for success in the test. Now it is arguably quite legitimate to approach a modest proportion of school learning in this fashion. Plausible examples may be found in physical education or foreign language programmes. Yet most school subjects cannot be translated into explicit test-related procedures without serious losses and distortions. Teachers being honest about the kind of learning they intend would in effect be signalling to children that they should not bother to try to 'understand'. Pupils would gather that they should ignore the challenge of developing properly connected knowledge and the applicability of such knowledge to a variety of circumstances. They would be persuaded to concentrate instead on managing specified tasks in a restricted range of contexts. Such a focus fails to reflect an adequate conception of knowledge, even if we judge knowledge worth having only according to what will help workers serving an industrial economy. Children may, for instance, learn to aim for a thin rule-bound grasp of mathematics. As a result they may often be unable to make any proper use of it in their lives, and they are likely to develop and retain negative attitudes to the subject.

David Blunkett certainly fails to grasp this point. For at the CBI President's Reception address in July 1999 he said:

> There are those who say that our focus on literacy is a threat to creativity ... It is precisely because we want pupils to think for themselves and to develop their creativity that we have set our target at Level 4 – reading and writing well – rather than at a basic level.

It simply has not occurred to him that 'Level 4' is in effect defined by Government policy as a test performance rather than as a clear description of real and valued personal qualities. The development of creativity, for instance is very difficult to reconcile with the growing practice of making learning objectives explicit at the outset of lessons, and the linking of these objectives with test performances.

To sum up, the traditional view of the damaging nature of teaching to the test holds good. The immediate consequence is a distortion and narrowing of the curriculum in the direction of the achievement of specific performances in a restricted range of contexts. Attempts by examiners to improve the variety of test questions introduce an element of luck into the proceedings. If the results of the tests are used to judge the effectiveness of teachers and schools this is an unhappy development.

To escape these difficulties, the assessment of pupil learning should not be used to hold schools and teachers to account. We need to develop other forms of accountability. I make a few remarks about this at the end of the pamphlet.

3
The official language of the National Curriculum and of the 'Standards' laid down for Newly Qualified Teachers

> *Using standardised language for accountability purposes distorts learning*

I will argue that standard languages are flawed, given the accountability purposes they are being expected to serve. I show that they cannot be used consistently by a range of users in a diversity of contexts unless they only capture 'thin' and restricted pupil performances. Consistent interpretation of such languages prevents them from characterising the kind of rich and connected knowledge and understanding which schools and higher education institutions should be promoting. Such knowledge is typically manifestable in an indefinite variety of ways. It does not comprise a limited number of kinds of performances in a confined range of contexts.

I turn now to the detailed development of this argument. The National Curriculum for England and Wales provides official descriptions of pupil achievement. Here are two examples. In science, pupils must be able to 'recognise the need for fair tests, describing, or showing in the way they perform their task, how to vary one factor whilst keeping others the same' (DFE 1995a). Pupils' writing must be 'varied and interesting, conveying meaning clearly in a range of forms for different readers, using a more formal style where appropriate' (DFE 1995b). Either of these descriptions should have a clear and constant meaning, whether applied to a child in a school in Newcastle upon Tyne or in Cornwall. Behind this move is the apparently admirable desire for a common language in which children's learning can be described.

Much National Curriculum language is intended to capture knowledge of a general and sometimes abstract character. By its very nature this knowledge could be demonstrated by pupils in many different ways in a range of contexts. Consider a few examples:

> [Pupils] make a range of contributions which show that they have listened perceptively and are sensitive to the development of discussion. (DFE 1995b)

> Pupils understand relative frequency as an estimate of probability and use this to compare outcomes of experiments. (DFE 1995c)

> [Pupils] use knowledge about how a specific mixture, such as salt and water, or sand and water, can be separated to suggest ways in which other similar mixtures might be separated. (DFE 1995a)

The Teacher Training Agency has drawn up lists of 'Standards' which students must acquire before they are awarded Qualified Teacher Status. These include 'identifying clear teaching objectives and content, appropriate to the subject matter and the pupils being taught, and specifying how these will be taught and assessed' and setting 'high expectations for pupils' behaviour, establishing and maintaining a good standard of discipline through well focused teaching and through positive and productive relationships' (DfEE 1998).

This appears to imply that schools wishing to employ Newly Qualified Teachers will have a clear and precise idea of what these teachers know, understand and can do in the classroom, whether they come from a School Centred Initial Teacher Training Course, the University of Durham or Manchester Metropolitan, to name three 'providers' at random. The OFSTED Inspection Guidance Handbook offers similar criteria by which teacher performance will be judged.

If these standard languages can function adequately, they provide a key element in the current strategy to hold schools, teachers and higher education institutions to account for the learning outcomes of their pupils and to compare the effectiveness of such institutions on this basis. Consider an extract from level 5 of Attainment Target 2 'Number and Algebra' from the Mathematics version of the National Curriculum: 'Pupils understand and use an appropriate non-calculator method for solving problems that involve multiplying and dividing any three digit number by any two digit number' (DFE 1995c).

At first sight, this may be interpreted in various ways. It does not say which non-calculator method pupils must use. There are in fact a number of possibilities. Moreover, 'problems' could cover very different kinds of challenges. These could include numerical questions written on paper in vertical format, but also practical tasks in realistic contexts that need among other things multiplication or division for successful completion. 'Understand and use' again could mean any of several different kinds of application. How is the teacher to judge whether the pupil method is 'appropriate'? Does this imply that there are certain approved methods, or that appropriateness is to be judged according to the context and the problem?

Can we rule out this range of possible interpretations? Mere translations of the official attainment descriptions are not going to help. For these will also be general and could be read in various ways. So why not opt for the obvious solution and offer examples?

Some teachers think that Standard Assessment Tasks provide these, thereby clarifying the meaning of the general descriptions of pupil attainments. Hence on this view the 'right answer' to a relevant SAT question tells us for instance what it is to know and understand the use of an appropriate non-calculator method. Another source of examples is the QCA, formerly SCAA . They now produce 'Exemplification of Standards' booklets containing illustrations of pupil work to represent particular level descriptions.

Just how might this turn out in practice? A teacher wonders whether one of her own pupils can 'understand and use an appropriate non-calculator method for solving problems that involve multiplying and dividing any three digit number by any two digit number.' She consults a SAT response or a SCAA exemplar, and decides whether her own pupil's work resembles the standard example adequately. There is unlikely to be an exact match. Or again, she ponders whether her pupil 'can construct pie charts' (DFE 1995c). Any standard example of such a construction probably will not match her pupil's construction perfectly. Indeed, it would seem ridiculous to insist on any kind of literal matching. So, even here, the teacher will have to judge whether the match between the standard example and her pupil's performance is sufficiently close.

Now without exact matching to standard examples, how are we to obtain a consistent interpretation of National Curriculum language across different teachers and schools? There are several 'appropriate' non-calculator methods for multiplying and dividing any three digit number by any two digit number. The standard example would only illustrate one of these. Moreover it would have to be entirely explicit about what was to count as 'understand and use'. 'Understand and use' is a complex and abstract idea that could be realised in practice in very many ways. If teachers cash this in a particular fashion, its richness and appropriate complexity is lost. Yet the standard example would have to illustrate just one version of 'understand and use' or teachers have scope to interpret their own pupil's performance. If the latter happens, teachers may differ in their interpretations. Hence the relevant attainment statement may not be used consistently by different teachers and schools.

Certainly the meaning of much National Curriculum language would be appreciably distorted if it were explained in terms of crude and superficial correspondences between a pupil's performance and a standard example. Language that is supposed to convey in general terms what pupils know, understand and can do would come to mean something quite different. It would declare in terms of primitive externals how pupil performances resembled a standard example in a portfolio, or a 'good answer' to a relevant SAT question.

Would anyone in their right mind lay down an equivalence between a general statement about attainment and just *one* illustrative task or SAT response? Surely the standard portfolio should rather contain a suitable *range* of tasks that would capture much more of the richness of the original statement. Although this move in some ways seems promising, problems remain. To be credited with the relevant statement of attainment, would pupils have to match performances with *all* the different exemplars? Or only some of them? Just how many different kinds of standard tasks should there be? How do we decide on the extent of the diversity? Suppose pupils did poorly on some and rather better on the others purportedly relating to the same attainment statement. How would this be judged?

Are these merely practical difficulties? I think not. The distortion of the meaning of standard statements about pupils' achievements would remain. We would not know how great a range of kinds of items to include, and neither would we have a secure justification for selecting any particular range. The whole idea of choosing kinds of items is open to the difficulties relating to 'similarity' discussed in an earlier section. Many of the National Curriculum statements about knowledge and understanding simply cannot be translated without loss into statements about how a given pupil performance resembles even several standard examples. Yet this is the proposal under discussion for ensuring that standard National Curriculum language is used consistently.

This matters a good deal because a consistently functioning standard language is a necessary condition for holding schools and teachers to account. Inconsistency introduces a significant element of unfairness when schools are compared according to their pupils' performance as characterised in this language. The consistency problem can be 'solved'. However, the solution twists the language so that it signifies superficial imitations of standard examples. This is quite unacceptable.

4
Using assessment to hold schools and teachers to account

> *Using assessment to hold schools and teachers to account is unjust.*

Test and examination performance is known to be correlated with the socio-economic status of the pupils. Other factors too may influence pupil performance, factors over which schools have no control. An increasingly popular idea is that such effects must be discounted if we are to use assessment results to inform fair judgements about the effectiveness of schools and teachers. Accordingly pupils are tested on starting school. This is known as baseline assessment. The theory is that we can find out what they know at the age of four. If we also measure what they know when they leave school at 11, we can discover how much they have learned in the interim. Taking account of background features, using indicators such as the number of children on free school meals, we can judge how much a school is doing for its pupils in comparison with other schools *who are teaching similar pupils*. This is the basic perspective within which so-called added value measures are developed. OFSTED school inspections purport to take account of the attainment levels of pupils on entry, and to judge the effectiveness of schools by considering subsequent attainment levels in the light of entry performance.

Attempts to measure added value represent well-intentioned departures from the use of crude results to judge the worth of schools. Yet there are serious problems. The notion of 'similarity' is at the heart of some of the difficulties. Common sense suggests several aspects of a school's catchment that are likely to affect how readily the pupils will learn. These will include whether the children are cold and hungry at home, whether they have enough sleep, how much conversation they have with their parents and the level of their parents' education. So we can try to compare the progress of a particular set of pupils with lots of other sets of pupils at schools where the above factors correspond closely. The trouble is that we simply do not know about all the factors that may affect learning progress, and hence cannot control for them when we try to make comparisons with similar schools. Such factors may be complex and unstable. Possibilities not always considered include subtle environmental pollution effects, or cultural factors specific to an area that are not identified by superficial attributions of socio-economic status.

Note that complex and elusive forces might affect the *initial baseline scores*. For instance, some middle class parents may act so as to prepare children for the initial tests. Yet this preparation may not be common to all parents apparently in this category, and the preparation may not be an explicit process. It could relate to aspects of conversation and play shared by child and parent. There might be no way of identifying which parents were offering the richer stimulation concerned. The nature of the resulting challenge for the school seeking to add value is not easy to predict. It seems that it could either make it harder, or easier! On the one hand some children might have been given a flying start by their parents. Hence once in school they might progress more quickly than similar children in other schools. So their school would unfairly be given extra credit. On the other hand, it might actually be *more difficult* for their school to be seen to add value given the quality of the pre-school input and the resulting high baseline scores. To repeat, we know too little and this ignorance does not seem to be a temporary difficulty.

Added-value experts recognise that there will be chance variations between the progress of apparently comparable cohorts of pupils, and that these variations must be added to the built in error that any test will have, however cleverly designed. So schools would have to be scrutinised over several years for more robust judgements to be made about their effectiveness. Yet much may change about a school over time. Some staff may leave, and others join. The head might be replaced. Individual teachers will vary in their energy, motivation and competence from year to year. Some schools have significant proportions of pupils who join them from elsewhere and only stay for a short period. What precisely is meant by 'the school'?

It is worth noting another problem about 'value added'. Its defenders assume that we can simply appeal to common sense in order to choose exit assessments that probe the same knowledge or subject matter as that dealt with by the baseline assessments. For instance, four year olds are tested on their grasp of mathematics. At eleven, another test is given, which is believed to check how much more *mathematics* the children know. Hence we can judge the performance of a given school in comparison with others teaching similar pupils mathematics. At least, this is what some people appear to think.

The assumption that we just know which exit tests are relevant may be questioned. Suppose a school does what some would regard as a fine job of mathematics teaching. The curriculum covers much in the way of basic skills, concepts, and learning of number facts. In addition, significant time is given to using and applying these basic building blocks in a diversity of contexts. There is a substantial element of problem-solving and investigation.

Now it is at least possible that officially sanctioned exit tests will fail to probe the results of this rich curriculum. The school might believe that it is adding to the 'mathematics value' that the pupils demonstrated on entry. Yet this could be missed by the allegedly relevant exit tests. Were a subtly different mathematics exit test to be employed, our school might be 'shown' to be doing better in comparison with other schools in similar circumstances with similar pupils. Or worse. Yet, to repeat, all the proposed exit tests may *appear* to be about *mathematics*.

To sum up, it is not possible in principle to justify the use of a particular exit test as part of a value added measure with a specified baseline test. Yet Standard Assessment Tasks and public examinations are integral features of current conceptions of value added measures, and these measures are at the heart of the current accountability regime as exemplified for instance by OFSTED. I conclude that the use of added value measures in this kind of way *for external accountability purposes* should be abandoned.

Giving data to schools themselves about their performance on specific tests and how this compares with apparently similar schools, a policy pursued by projects such as ALIS and PIPs[3] is a very different matter. Schools could be aware of the frailty of the information coming to them, but still make sensitive use of it in their own particular contexts. If cost permitted data could be offered on schools' value added measures according to several different exit tests and teachers could weigh for themselves the relevance of the potentially conflicting results.

5
Prescribing teaching methods

> *Teachers are being told how to teach and yet are still being held to account for their pupils' learning.*

To the extent that Government requires teachers to use certain approaches in the classroom, they cannot at the same time hold teachers to account for the learning outcomes of their pupils. On the other hand, if teachers can still make professional decisions about how to adapt approved methods to their particular circumstances it becomes unclear that they are using any particular methods, whether approved or otherwise.

The Department for Education and Employment and the Teacher Training Agency are increasingly prescriptive about the methods and approaches teachers should use in the classroom. This is especially apparent in the primary sector. The National Literacy and Numeracy

Strategies provide ideal lesson structures, recommend proportions of whole class teaching, and even among other things suggest seating arrangements. Teachers are told that these methods are not compulsory. However, if OFSTED thinks that the results of schools departing from approved methods are unsatisfactory then those without an adequate explanation are likely to be severely criticised in their Inspection Reports.

This level of intervention is quite unprecedented. In the early days of the National Curriculum, Government ministers took a pride in asserting that although Government was now in the 'secret garden' of the curriculum, and legislating about what should be taught, they were (of course) leaving it to the professionals to decide how to teach. It is now felt that available research evidence shows specific teaching approaches to be the most effective in bringing about learning and that this justifies intervening in the approaches teachers adopt in the classroom.

We are currently bombarded by advertisements for so-called Literacy Consultants and Numeracy Consultants. Many of these consultants will be asked to provide demonstration lessons as part of their duties. These will be observed by class teachers from the relevant Local Education Authorities. The implication of this is that the experts can show the officially approved methods over the space of a lesson or two.

Some teachers and commentators on the educational scene object to teachers being treated as mere technicians. It is believed that teachers should be viewed as professionals, and that they will especially deplore being told how to teach by agencies some of whose key members have never actually taught in a school. However, this attitude may not cut much ice with policy makers eager to raise standards in the basics, and concerned by what they regard as the UK's lamentable position in international comparisons of pupil attainment in subjects such as literacy and numeracy. If we know what works, it will be said, then we really ought to teach on this basis, and not allow ourselves to become precious about teachers' dignity and status.

Examples of methods being prescribed include the following: arrange the classroom in a horseshoe shape around an appropriately positioned overhead projector; divide children into sets by attainment; teach phonics in a specific way; bring children together at the end of a lesson for a plenary session in which themes arising from the body of the lesson are drawn together and consolidated.

Much of this may seem perfectly acceptable at first sight. However, to the extent that teachers are being forced to adopt official methods they should not be held accountable for the learning outcomes of their pupils. Instead, the designers of the National Literacy and Numeracy Strategies should be blamed if results are not as good as they should be (whatever that might mean). Equally, if results are splendid then the method creators should receive every credit. (Though if 'results' simply means improved performance in public tests and examinations, then we should not get too excited in either case, as I argued earlier.)

Further, when we look closer at attempts to prescribe teaching methods, additional problems become apparent. Effective teaching, whether in the course of interaction with the whole class or smaller groups, seems bound to take account of the pupils' responses. This means that any particular lesson is to a degree unpredictable, even if a detailed plan embedded within the Literacy or Numeracy Strategy is being used. The teacher has to gauge minute by minute the level of her children's interest and motivation and the extent to which they are understanding. She continually modifies her style of explanation, tone, timing and organisation accordingly. For instance a primary teacher might deviate significantly from the lesson structures and timings encouraged by the Literacy and Numeracy Strategies. That is why one teacher's lesson on a particular topic may differ significantly from another's, even if the same content and similar age and attainment groupings of pupils are involved. It is less and less clear, once the realistic detail is taken into account, what method is common to all the teachers.

Perhaps some prescriptions, such as putting the children in a horseshoe arrangement, have a clearer and more robust meaning whatever the teaching context. However, even this approach would be modified by any sane teachers in certain situations. It will still depend on the shape of the classroom, it will still need to take account of the idiosyncrasies of particular pupils or groups, and so on. If the authorities insist that teachers should not think for themselves, but implement officially approved methods come what may, then we return to the earlier point. If teachers should not try to use their own judgement but adopt the official approaches, then to that extent the teachers themselves cannot be held directly responsible for whether their pupils are learning. The Government, the Teacher Training Agency or their equivalent cannot have it both ways.

Despite claims by Government agencies to be in possession of indisputable evidence for the worth of certain approaches, it is worth reminding ourselves of the difficulty of obtaining such evidence. Researchers could compare, for example, classrooms in which children are arranged in a horseshoe shape around an OHP with classrooms in which children are not so arranged. The point would be to measure the effect of the horseshoe configuration on learning outcomes. To do this it would be important to ensure that there were no other features peculiar to teachers and classrooms involved in this kind of approach. For instance, it might turn out that quite independently teachers keen to work in this way happen to be good at helping the children to perform well in the tests that measure the outcomes. To eliminate this possible influence on the results the classrooms concerned need to vary in as many other respects as can be contrived. The classrooms with horseshoe arrangements ought to vary in the same kinds of ways as the classrooms without such arrangements. Otherwise the comparisons between the learning in the 'horseshoe' classrooms and the others may be flawed. However, there is a general difficulty about being sure we have pinned down all the relevant variables in an exercise of this kind. To meet all these challenges is a tall order indeed.

6
OFSTED inspections

> *OFSTED inspections cannot accurately detect teaching quality.*

Some features of a school or a teaching situation can be readily detected by an outside observer, even on the basis of relatively brief inspection. These have been referred to as *compliance issues*. Does the school obey Health and Safety regulations? Is the school coming together for an act of worship each day? Is there a Child Protection Policy? Does the school have up-to-date policies for the various subjects? There are also factual points to which the school can provide straightforward answers for inspectors. These include patterns of school attendance, performance on compulsory national tests, school accommodation, staffing and so on. Note a third set of negative features that do seem to be directly observable. Pupils might be unruly, violent, prone to speak when the teacher or other pupils are speaking, liable to make a great deal of noise, or directly disobedient.

Admittedly there is some scope for differences of interpretation between inspectors here.

The criteria for inspection in the OFSTED handbook cover many of these aspects of schools and classrooms. They are mixed together without apology or explanation with very different issues relating to teaching quality and whether the school provides 'value for money'. Many questions have been raised about the consistency or reliability with which inspectors are able to make judgements about this fourth class of issues. Carol Fitz-Gibbon has led the way (Fitz-Gibbon 1996). OFSTED appears unruffled by these criticisms, and blandly gestures at various aspects of the inspection process that they feel are bound to make inspections reliable.

There should be no difficulty about reaching reliable verdicts on compliance or factual issues. The challenge for inspectors is to achieve reliability when they make judgements about teaching quality. School reports are riddled with confident and authoritative pronouncements of this kind. Inspectors are required to assess whether, for instance 'teachers set expectations so as to challenge pupils and deepen their knowledge and understanding'. The Handbook (OFSTED 1995) states that teaching methods include 'exposition, explanation, demonstration, discussion, practical activity, investigation, testing and problem-solving'. Inspectors have to judge how far teachers are using these methods 'effectively'. This is defined as 'the extent to which [the methods] extend or deepen pupils' knowledge and understanding and develop their skills' (OFSTED 1995:69).

For the sake of argument let us grant that the average OFSTED inspector is an experienced professional, accustomed to observing teaching and with knowledge of the age groups concerned. We may also assume, as the OFSTED handbook indicates, that the evidence available to the inspector goes well beyond the simple observation of a few lessons. Inspectors can look at the children's work, they can question the pupils, they can scrutinise the longer term planning in which the observed lessons are embedded, and they can compare pupils' current written work with that being produced at the beginning of that academic year or at some other useful point in time.

Yet none of this goes anywhere near to justifying inspectors' confidence in their authoritative verdicts on the effectiveness of the teaching. Presumably any given lesson is to be judged on the basis of whether by the end of it children have learned what was intended. Now perhaps an inspector could make an informed judgement on the teaching of very specific skills such as those developed sometimes in a PE session to thirty children or more. However, to describe this inspection task as challenging would be an understatement. Moreover, in the vast majority of cases such informed judgements are *not* feasible. If the lesson aspires to develop children's 'connected' understanding, this cannot be assessed by means of the limited evidence available to the most perceptive of inspectors. It would be difficult even to check whether just one pupil had learned in this rich fashion as a result of the teaching observed.

Furthermore, especially in the case of younger children learning abstract subjects such as mathematics and science, 'connected' knowledge grows slowly and erratically. It is rarely appropriate for the teacher to think in terms of specific elements of knowledge which children will obtain as a result of a lesson or so. Inspectors certainly should not assume that most lessons contribute to learning in a way that fits this short term paradigm. If the *teacher* insisted on thinking in this fashion, perhaps because of perceived pressure from OFSTED, the effect would be to distort the intended learning in the direction of narrowly conceived skills which could be quickly taught and which the children could only exercise in the kinds of contexts in which they were acquired. To reiterate an earlier point, this is not the kind of knowledge that would stand them in good stead in their future as workers in a competitive industrial economy.

I suggest that OFSTED's real approach differs dramatically from that suggested by their rhetoric. They have *already decided* which methods are effective. Normally they do not feel that they need to observe learning outcomes. This is just as well, given that they are not usually in a position to assess whether children have acquired the knowledge intended for them. If inspectors were honest with the schools and teachers they inspect, they would admit that what they are *really* trying to do is to discover whether teachers are using the approved methods.

They can speak with apparent sophistication and sensitivity to teachers' professionalism in passages such as this:

> The choice of teaching methods and organisational strategies is a matter for the school and the teacher's discretion. This should be based upon the objectives of the lesson and factors such as the number of pupils, their age, attainment and behaviour, and the nature of the resources and accommodation. (OFSTED 1995:69)

They begin to give the game away by going on to say:

> The key to the judgement is whether the methods and organisation are fit for the purpose of achieving high standards of work and behaviour.

Just so. But how will they know that?

> Direct evidence will come from lesson observation. Scrutiny of pupils' work and discussion with teachers and pupils gives evidence over a longer time scale of whether methods and organisation are sufficiently responsive to the range of curricular objectives and pupils' needs. (*ibid*:69)

However, the 'evidence' available even to the most perceptive and observant inspector simply could not justify a judgement about such matters. It is difficult enough for an experienced head observing a teacher over a period of a year or so to know how far her particular approaches are responsible for children's learning. After all, to judge fairly that a teacher is *causing* her children to learn in a certain way an inspector would need to know that the specific approach used would bring about a similar result with a group of similar children in any relevantly similar context. Such knowledge is simply not available. We do not know enough about the variables affecting learning to be clear about what counts as 'similar'. Even if a generously funded research project could solve some of these problems, with hosts of observers, and an exhaustive study of the range of variables that may impinge on learning outcomes, there is no doubt that such research has never been carried out. Even if it had, individual OFSTED inspectors could not bring its fruits to bear on the appraisal of specific lessons.

Moreover, establishing that teachers are *causing* the children to learn is not sufficient. Even if this could be demonstrated, which it could not, the inspector would also need to be clear from the evidence that the teacher has not achieved a 'lucky' success. The teacher must *intend* the specific learning allegedly detected by the inspector. She must believe that her particular methods are likely to bring about the learning, and on the basis of a brief observation the inspector must be able to *see* that these methods are being used.

This could be just part of a judgement that, for example, the teacher has some kind of 'ability' or 'competence' at choosing and putting into effect methods and organisation 'fit for the purposes of achieving high standards of work and behaviour.' OFSTED must hold that inspectors can make judgements about competences in this fashion, or from their point of view the judgements about teaching quality are pointless. While they talk disarmingly about 'snapshots' and the fact that the lessons seen may not be a representative sample of that teacher's work, they do *grade* teachers. This grade is not simply meant to refer to what inspectors 'actually see'. If it were, schools might be forgiven for taking relatively little notice of it.

> Teaching should not be viewed in isolation from its impact. How effectively pupils are learning and the progress they make is a response to the teaching. The emphasis of this section of the report will be on teaching evaluated in relation to the criteria in the Framework, but you should draw on the evidence of pupils' progress wherever possible to exemplify its effectiveness. It is of little help to the school or parents simply to re-iterate the criteria; you need to identify and exemplify *what works and what doesn't* and how it is seen in pupils' learning. OFSTED Web-site advice to inspectors.
>
> (From OFSTED Web-site advice to inspectors. Updated version available at: http:/www.ofsted.gov.uk/pubs/inspect/81.htm]. [My italics]

Inspectors in short are supposed to be able to detect whether teachers have abilities that could be exercised in a range of classrooms and contexts. It is or would be disingenuous of inspectors to pretend that they are only grading 'what they see'. Yet on the evidence available, they are not entitled to arrive at verdicts about such 'abilities'. Nor is it clear that teachers who seem to perform effectively in some contexts will perform well in others. This is a matter of common professional experience. Admittedly some teachers are so inadequate personally that they will perform badly in virtually any context. A few other favoured stars are brilliant with any age group, in any subject and in any school. The vast majority may seem very 'effective' in some contexts, with some groups of children and when teaching some subjects, but not with others.

The observed unreliability of inspectors' verdicts on teaching quality seems to be entirely understandable in the light of this discussion. This is not a technical problem, which OFSTED could solve by improving their procedures. They are trying to do something which *in principle cannot* be achieved reliably.

Note on the Standards required for Newly Qualified Teachers

The argument of earlier sections may be applied to the Standards laid down by the Teacher Training Agency for Qualified Teacher Status (QTS). Neither university nor school-based tutors are in any better position to judge whether students are bringing about intended learning than are OFSTED inspectors when supposedly grading 'effective' teaching.

If we retain OFSTED's definition of 'effective teaching', it is clear that even several observations cannot enable tutors to judge securely whether students 'ensure effective teaching of whole classes, and of groups and individuals within the whole class setting, so that teaching objectives are met' or whether they 'evaluate their own teaching critically and use this to improve their effectiveness' (DfEE 1998). Other aspects of classroom style may more easily be probed, such as whether they 'establish and maintain a purposeful working atmosphere' or 'establish a safe environment' (*ibid.*) (though there is some scope for subjective value judgements here.)

It follows from this that trainers are in effect being expected to identify whether students are exhibiting the 'methods that work' in their performances. That is rather unfortunate given that as we saw earlier many of these methods are either empty or hugely difficult to justify conclusively on the basis of firm evidence. Of course, this is made no plainer in the rhetoric of the Standards than it is in the criteria for effective teaching in the OFSTED handbook.

On the face of it, many of the Standards are not wholly objectionable. Many would agree that at least some of the time it is desirable that students

> use teaching methods which sustain the momentum of pupils' work and keep all pupils engaged through structuring information well, including outlining content and aims, signalling transitions and summarising key points as the lesson progresses. (DfEE 1998)

The trouble is that, as we saw earlier, there are many ways of interpreting this. In order to obtain consistency superficial and misleading symptoms of the 'methods that work' would be sought by assessors, whether intentionally or otherwise. For if students were making flexible and intelligent teaching decisions according to the circumstances and the responses of pupils the 'methods that work' would prove singularly difficult to apprehend.

OFSTED checks whether training institutions have satisfactory Quality Assurance arrangements. These are supposed to determine whether relevant tutors can consistently apply OFSTED or TTA criteria to student classroom performances. The result of all this is that students are going to have to 'show that they are doing it' just as candidates taking driving tests glance ostentatiously in the mirror to satisfy the examiner. The real learning of pupils does not seem to figure much in this process (but fortunately it still may occur at times, whether or not it is intended or observed).

Moreover, again as was argued earlier, success in one classroom context need not transfer to another even when there seem obvious parallels between the second and the first. Hence attributing to a student the 'ability' to 'ensure effective teaching of whole classes', for example, would involve the invocation of a dangerously mythological psychological trait.

To sum up, the current system seems destined to fail some students who might make 'good' teachers, and to pass others who should never be allowed near young learners. Awarding Qualified Teacher Status has never been, and could never be, a foolproof process. However, the current Quality Assurance mechanisms and the language of the Standards make things much worse than they need to be. There are alternative approaches, and these are touched on in the following section.

7
Realistic accountability: Can we still hold teachers and schools to account? If so how, and why?

Some policy makers will dismiss my whole approach. 'You are unrealistic!' they will complain. 'Education is very expensive! Our current accountability process may be far from perfect, but it is the best we can do. What are you going to put in its place?'

There is no easy answer. However, I believe that there *are* genuine alternatives to current policy. Consider the question of making schools accountable. How can society at large ensure that schools are putting the money entrusted to them to good use? I would argue that it is possible in at least three relatively uncomplicated ways for schools to be scrutinised. I draw on Section 6's discussion of inspection in my explanation. The suggestions are not original, *and to some extent they form part of present practice.* Their effectiveness should not be underestimated.

First, inspectors can continue to check whether schools are complying with relevant legislation. This can cover anything from the approach to pupil exclusions and the probity of the schools' finances to the way in which School Governors are carrying out their statutory functions.

Second, relevant factual matters can be determined, such as the state of repair of the buildings, the quality and extent of equipment and resources and the number of children on free school meals. Inspectors can take note if, for instance only half of the Year 6 pupils in a primary school seem to be able to read, or if a significant minority of a Year 11 set are unable to perform simple calculations. These only need to be crude and broad brush judgements. Some warning signs may be so glaringly obvious that no reasonable observer could ignore them.

Inspectors can also ask the following questions during any school visit. Broadly speaking, do the pupils seem to be gaining knowledge and understanding? Do they seem to be developing their minds appropriately, and at a level to be expected from their age group in their context? I believe that inspectors can make perfectly acceptable judgements at this level of generality about what they see. This is possible without any attempts to 'detect' complex pupil learning on the basis of brief observation, or to provide reliable fine-grained judgements about teaching quality, whether on seven point scales or otherwise. The broader judgements I am supporting are certainly fallible but could still be useful when understood as having such modest status.

Third, inspectors can discover by means of quite limited visits whether key negative elements are present within the school situation. For instance a total breakdown of discipline may be readily detected. Or again, a discrepancy between attendance as indicated on school registers and the actual numbers of pupils in school may easily be identified. I once worked in a school where there were far more children on the registers than there were genuine pupils. School

Inspectors eventually discovered this (though it took them some time).

If these three areas were covered by inspectors this could form part of a rigorous and comprehensive type of accountability. However, objectors will claim that it fails to grasp the nettle of teaching quality. In Sections 1 and 6 it has in effect been argued that quality *cannot* be measured by the devices embedded within current policy. Now if quality is no longer defined directly in terms that incorporate pupil learning outcomes it needs an alternative interpretation. I suggest that quality should include a reference to matters of value or principle. These value issues ultimately would be defended by an appeal to fundamental educational aims. It certainly should not be left to teachers and other education professionals to determine these values and aims. Similarly it is not the exclusive prerogative of doctors to decide the values underlying the prioritising of scarce NHS resources. This pamphlet cannot discuss basic educational aims in the detail they deserve. It can, however *suggest* desirable features of learning contexts which could be sought by inspectors.

Are the children gaining experience of working together? Do these experiences involve the pupils in valuing each other's contributions and respecting individual differences in terms of culture and religion? Are they encouraged to understand what they are being taught, rather than simply to absorb it and memorise it? Are pupils invited to question and to examine critically material offered by teachers? Are they invited to develop intellectual curiosity and do they have opportunities to follow up their curiosity with teacher support? Are they being introduced to a range of ideas and of subjects to whet their appetite for more? Are they being prepared for their role as citizens of a democracy? Are they having lessons in which they are encouraged to compare democratic forms of government with other kinds? Are they examining what it is to have a religious faith, and the key features of the main world religions? Are the pupils for the most part enjoying their learning?

Relationships in schools, between staff and pupils, and between the various adults within the institution, can also be scrutinised with reference to key values. Questions that can be addressed include the following. Are managers treating staff with respect? Is there genuine consultation when policy issues are decided? Do teaching staff treat children with respect? Are school rules reviewed regularly in consultation with staff, pupils and parents? What is the quality of the partnership between School Governors and School Staff? Is the school discipline policy implemented fairly and effectively?

Either OFSTED inspectors or old-style HMI can discover whether schools and other educational institutions are working in accordance with such principles. The kind of evidence required, and the judgements that would result, should not provoke the fundamental questions about reliability and accuracy of inspections discussed in Section 6 above. Nor do they need to rely on approaches to the assessment of learning outcomes that are so open to criticism. This version of accountability is far from being neat and tidy. Yet it could be fair to the teachers and pupils concerned. In a real sense it could play a crucial role in raising standards.

If accountability became acceptable in the terms just outlined, teacher trainers, whether school or university-based, could also be encouraged to work with students in a similar way. They too could judge issues of compliance and relevant factual matters. They could detect the absence of key negative features when scrutinising student performance in the classroom. While no pretence would be made to ascertain the precise extent to which pupils were learning from students in particular lessons, tutors could still offer broader verdicts on whether children seemed to be learning. (If we are honest, this is what has happened in the past, and it is very difficult to see what else can be done in the space of teaching placements lasting a few weeks.) The kinds of values and principles outlined above could be sought within the range of practices exhibited by students during school placements.

Accordingly OFSTED or the equivalent could examine how far teacher-training partnerships are effective in making judgements of this kind. Efforts to secure pseudo-scientific consistency of judgements by means of allegedly sophisticated quality assurance mechanisms could be abandoned. Equally, the pretence that we know the 'methods that work' and that school partnerships can detect students using them would be forsaken.

Finally, many have advocated the virtues of institutional self-evaluation. Schools and colleges are encouraged to develop systems of self-review in which they regularly and rigorously judge their own progress and performance against targets they have set themselves. However, the role of self-evaluation in accountability has been sidelined recently by the harder-edged performance-based versions of accountability. A renewed emphasis on self-review could include statutory provision for the regular sharing of its fruits with external Government-sponsored agencies. It should be possible for schools and colleges to have intelligible and rigorous conversations about 'improvement' with inspectors and others that do not concentrate exclusively on 'effective' teaching as measured by learning outcomes. Admittedly the complexity and context-related aspects of 'improvement' would have to be understood by all parties. Society through its agencies including the Inspectorate could expect to influence the kinds of targets which educational institutions set themselves. A broad framework of values and principles could and should be shared by educational institutions and the external agencies to which they are rendering an account. Within this framework the institutions can explain and justify the ways in which they are constantly seeking to improve their practice.

Notes

1. For evidence relating to the 'transfer' of mathematics learning see, for example, K. Ruthven's 'Ability stereotyping in mathematics' (1987) and the Assessment of Performance Unit's work on this subject, summarised in *A Review of Monitoring in Mathematics 1978 to 1982* (1985). A psychologist offering extensive evidence on this topic is S. J. Ceci. See, for instance, Ceci's *On Intelligence ... More or Less: A bio-ecological treatise on intellectual development* (1990) or 'The effects of context on cognition: Postcards from Brazil' by S. J. Ceci and A. Roazzi (1994).

2. The expression 'Mozart effect' is currently used to refer to empirical studies purporting to show that exposure to music boosts academic performance or IQ. It has been claimed that while the work of a variety of composers may prove helpful, Mozart is best. See, for instance, the brief untitled article by M. Gardiner, A. Fox, F. Knowles and D. Jeffrey in *Nature* (1996) about how exposure to a programme of music and art improved performance in mathematics.

3. ALIS, PIPs, YELLIS and other information systems are based at the Curriculum, Evaluation and Management Centre, Durham University. They claim to offer schools data about how their pupils' performance compares with that of similar pupils in similar schools.

References

Assessment of Performance Unit (1985), *A Review of Monitoring in Mathematics 1978 to 1982* (2 vols) (London, DES).

Ceci, S. J. (1990), *On Intelligence . . . More or Less: A bio-ecological treatise on intellectual development.* Englewood Cliffs, NJ: Prentice-Hall.

Ceci, S. J. and Roazzi, A. (1994), 'The effects of context on cognition: Postcards from Brazil' in R. J. Sternberg and R. K. Wagner (eds), *Mind in context: Interactionist perspectives on human intelligence,* pp.45-55. New York: Cambridge University Press.

Davis, A. (1988), 'Ability and learning'. *Journal of Philosophy of Education,* 22.1: 45-55.

DFE (1995a), *Science in the National Curriculum.* London: HMSO.

— (1995b), *English in the National Curriculum.* London: HMSO.

— (1995c), *Mathematics in the National Curriculum.* London: HMSO.

DfEE (1998), *Teaching: High Status, High Standards.* Circular 4/98. London: HMSO.

Fitz-Gibbon, C. (1996), *Monitoring Education.* London: Cassell.

Gardiner, M., Fox, A., Knowles, F. and Jeffrey, D. (1996), Untitled, *Nature,* 381.6580:284.

OFSTED (1995), *Guidance on the Inspection of Nursery and Primary Schools.* The OFSTED HANDBOOK. London: HMSO.

— (1998a), *The National Numeracy Project: An HMI evaluation.*

— (1998b) *Inspection Report on Witton Gilbert Primary School County Durham.*

QCA (1998), *Standards at key stage 2.* London: QCA.

Ruthven, K. (1987), 'Ability stereotyping in mathematics', *Educational Studies in Mathematics* (1988), 18:243- 253.

Times Educational Supplement (1999), Numbers help with the Words, 26 February.

Suggestions for further reading

I have tried hard to write this pamphlet in a straightforward style, avoiding technicalities and a drily academic approach. However, much of the material presented here is based on research which some readers may wish to follow up in publications designed for an academic audience.

Many of the themes are explored in more depth in my philosophical monograph Davis, A (1998), *The Limits of Educational Assessment*. Oxford: Blackwell. Some of my arguments are discussed by others in the following papers:

Winch, C. and Gingell, J. (1996), 'Educational assessment: reply to Andrew Davis', *Journal of Philosophy of Education*, 30.3:377-388.

Williams, K. (1998), 'Assessment and the challenge of scepticism' in D. Carr (ed.) *Education, Knowledge and Truth*. London: Routledge.

White, J. (1999), 'Thinking about assessment', *Journal of Philosophy of Education*, 33.2.

My objections to 'the methods that work' are developed more rigorously in my 'Prescribing teaching methods' to be published in the late autumn of 1999 in the *Journal of Philosophy of Education*, 33.3.

Topics of forthcoming titles from IMPACT

- Sex Education

- Education and Equality with special reference to school admissions

- Personal, Social and Health Education

- Performance Related Pay

- Citizenship Education

- The National Curriculum after 2000

- The Place of Modern Foreign Languages in the Curriculum

- Post-16 Vocational Education

- Good Teaching

If you would like to be put on a mailing list for further information about the publication of these pamphlets and about any symposia or other events connected with their launch, please contact

The Education Bookshop
20 Bedford Way, London WC1H 0AL
Telephone 0171 612 6050 Fax 0171 612 6407
Email: bmbc@ioe.ac.uk

Journal of Philosophy of Education

The Journal of the Philosophy of Education Society of Great Britain

Edited by Richard Smith

The *Journal of Philosophy of Education* publishes articles representing a wide variety of philosophical traditions. They vary from examination of fundamental philosophical issues in their connection with education, to detailed critical engagement with current educational policy from a philosophical point of view. The journal aims to promote rigorous thinking on educational matters and to identify and criticise the ideological forces shaping education.

Recent and forthcoming highlights:
Political Liberalism and Civic Education, Stephen Mulhall
Paternalism and Consent, Haley Richmond
Rorty's Conception of Education, Eliyahu Rosenow
Europe and the World of Learning, Padraig Hogan
Teaching Mathematics, Yvette Solomon
Sex Education, David Archard

Special Issues:
Values, Virtues and Violence: Education and the Public Understanding of Morality (1999)
The Limits of Educational Assessment (1998)
Illusory Freedoms: Liberalism, Education and the Market (1997)
Quality and Education (1996)

Journal of Philosophy of Education ISSN 0309-8249 Published in March, July and November
Subscription Rates, Vol. 33/1999:
Institutions: Europe £224, N. America $413, Rest of World £250.
Personal: Europe £72, N. America $140, Rest of World £85.

To subscribe to Journal of Philosophy of Education please use the order form on the Blackwell website: http://www.blackwellpublishers.co.uk, send an email to jnlinfo@blackwellpublishers.co.uk, or contact either of the following:

- Blackwell Publishers Journals, PO Box 805, 108 Cowley Road, Oxford OX4 1FH, UK. Tel: +44 (0)1865 244083, fax +44 (0)1865 381581
- Journals Marketing (JOPE), Blackwell Publishers, 350 Main Street, Malden, MA 02148, USA. Tel. +1 (781) 388 8200, fax +1 (781) 388 8210

SPECIAL OFFER for 1999 — **BLACKWELL** *Publishers*
Electronic access included in the institutional subscription price to the print edition
For more information visit our website

http://www.blackwellpublishers.co.uk

Join the

Philosophy of Education Society of Great Britain
and receive the
Journal of Philosophy of Education

FREE!

Formed in 1964, the Society exists to promote the study, teaching and application of Philosophy of Education. It holds an annual three-day conference as well as local branch meetings and conferences. Members receive the *Journal of Philosophy of Education* as part of the benefits of their annual membership.

Membership rates:

(worldwide) £24.00 (£12.00 unwaged; £8.00 non-Western income as determined by the Executive Committee). Payment by credit card possible (with £2.00 surcharge).

Membership enquiries: please contact

Dr Colin Wringe,
Department of Education
University of Keele
Staffordshire ST5 5BG UK

E-mail: eda26@cc.keele.ac.uk